Benjamin Bach

Implications of enabling technologies for Apple Inc.

Cybermarketing & enabling technologies

Benjamin Bach

Implications of enabling technologies for Apple Inc.

Cybermarketing & enabling technologies

GRIN Verlag

Bibliografische Information der Deutschen Nationalbibliothek: Die Deutsche Bibliothek verzeichnet diese Publikation in der Deutschen Nationalbibliografie; detaillierte bibliografische Daten sind im Internet über http://dnb.d-nb.de/ abrufbar.

1. Auflage 2007
Copyright © 2007 GRIN Verlag
http://www.grin.com/
Druck und Bindung: Books on Demand GmbH, Norderstedt Germany
ISBN 978-3-638-81096-8

UNIVERSITY OF
LINCOLN

MKG 109

ASSESSMENT
SEMESTER B
CYBERMARKETING

Summative Assessment

Benjamin Bach
MSc International Marketing Strategy
30th March 2007

Table of Contents

Table of Figures

1. Introduction

This report critically examines the implications of enabling technologies that will have an impact on the marketing strategies of businesses. As technology, such as the Internet, provides new opportunities and challenges for marketers while aligning a customer-focused strategy, this medium is becoming crucial in today's dynamic business environment in order to maintain competitive. This report analyses the role of the Internet for marketers followed by an examination of opportunities and threats to global businesses from enabling technologies. Furthermore, a detailed examination of strategic approaches will be given, focusing on the e-marketing mix and pricing strategies in order to highlight the increased pressures for organisations when applying new media formats. Apple Inc. will be indicative as an example for important aspects throughout the report, in order to clarify and visualise the execution of new media formats by Apple Inc., followed by a critical evaluation of their web site with a focus on strengths, weaknesses and proposed improvements.

2. The Role of the Internet for E-businesses & Marketers

According to Doole and Lowe (2004), the IT and communications technologies are growing at a tremendous velocity and have a major impact on the way global business is done. In particular the Internet facilitates the integration of different technologies. Nowadays, technology is a vital influence and underlines the choice of implementation strategies of the international marketing mix and furthermore, "enables the more effective control of a firm's diverse international activities" (Doole and Lowe, 2004, p.403). The Internet has had, and still has, a vast effect on international trade, as physical geographic boundaries are abrogated due to the increasing number of broadband penetrations and access to technologies. According to Internet World Stats (2007), 37.6m users are currently utilising the Internet in the UK, which is 62.3 per cent of the total UK population. Globally 1.1bn Internet users, equivalent to 16.9 per cent of the world's population, exploit the Internet that identifies a global growth rate of 208.7 per cent since the year 2000. This highlights that this medium is crucial to marketing in order to stay competitive in today's business dynamism. The role of the Internet for e-businesses and e-marketers includes critical opportunities and challenges when applying technologies to their businesses operations.

2.1 Opportunities & Advantages of Enabling Technologies

E-marketing provides a chance for business operations to be executed in a global marketplace, as it offers "an alternative route to market to traditional distribution channels" (Doole and Lowe, 2004, p.409). According to McDonald and Wilson (1999), cited in Chaffey *et al.* (2003), the paradigm shift between traditional and new media marketing approaches is inherently identified by six determinants.

2.1.1 Interactivity

As the customer or other stakeholder is initiating the contact by getting proactive, the company can and shall provide the individual with a huge information supply "without human interventions" (Sheth and Sharma, 2005, p.612), because according to Bickerton *et al.* (2001) the customer is in control. Furthermore, the personal needs and wants of the customer "can be addressed and taken into account in future dialogues" (Chaffey *et al.*, 2003, p.29) by encouraging a two-way communications loop. Interactivity is of vital importance, as it offers the customer an interesting and constantly changing basis for their Internet experience and curiosity.

2.1.2 Intelligence

According to McDonald and Wilson (1999), cited in Chaffey *et al.* (2003), "the Internet can be used as a relatively low-cost method of collecting marketing research" (p.29) especially about customers' or stakeholders' perceptions of tangible and intangible goods, or marketing and channel management effectiveness. For instance, Apple Inc. is able to profile their customers on the basis of information received in questionnaires or feedback features (Figure 1). This information can be used to enhance their products and services on- and offline and furthermore, assists in determining customer satisfaction. Marketing research intelligence can also be applied in tracking where the customers click on a particular web site using a "transaction log file" (p.29). This technology enables businesses "to respond in real time to buyer behaviour" (p.29), i.e. the customers.

4

Figure 1. Apple Inc.'s Feedback Service Feature

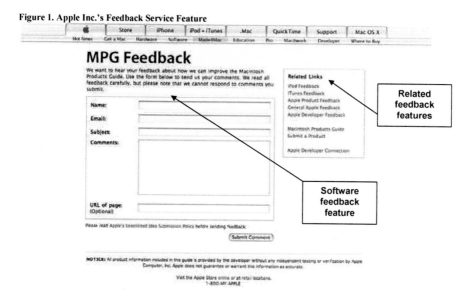

(Source: Adapted from www.apple.com/uk/, 2007)

2.1.3 Individualisation

The individual marketing communications message can be tailored to the needs and wants of the customer as opposed to "traditional media where the same message tends to be broadcast to everyone" (Chaffey *et al.*, 2003, p.29). This is an important aspect in achieving a customer relationship on a one-to-one basis, and setting up key accounts while categorising the customers in order to provide them with specifically tailored deals. This is particular important in satisfying specific personal needs and experiences which can be created "by customizing information for individual customers" (Sheth and Sharma, 2005, p.613), e.g. "My Account" feature of Apple Inc. where personalised product information will be displayed according to prior purchases (Figure 2). Furthermore, the degree of customisation can be "controlled either by the firm or by the customer" (Mohammed *et al.*, 2003, p.16) in order to provide to optimal two-way communications flow.

5

Figure 2: Apple Inc.'s Customised "My Account" Feature

(Source: Adapted from www.apple.com/uk/, 2007)

2.1.4 Integration

Integration provides a crucial attribute in communicating on virtual and physical media formats, as this determines the optimal mix of a company's marketing communications. The Internet can be used, according to Chaffey *et al.* (2003), as a "direct-response tool, enabling customers to respond to offers and promotions publicised in other media" (p.31) such as television or newspaper (Figure 3). Furthermore, the Internet can support the buying decision by offering phone numbers to receive product information or assistance in placing an order, e.g. Apple Inc.'s customer service helpline (Figure 4) and customer support section (Figure 5). Integration of on- and offline marketing communications can be used to track purchases done and hence, help to enhance the whole service landscape for customers or stakeholders. Furthermore, the Internet provides communication improvements to all stakeholders in contrast to the traditional media, as instant communication is possible via to email or electronic data interchanges.

Figure 3: Apple Inc.'s iPod Print Advertisement

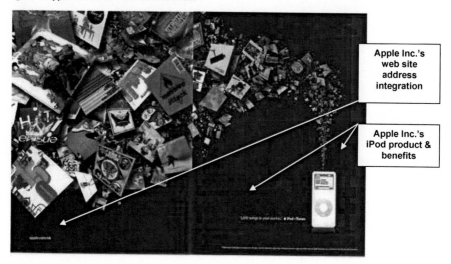

Apple Inc.'s web site address integration

Apple Inc.'s iPod product & benefits

(Source: Adapted from www.creativeclub.co.uk/, 2007)

Figure 4: Apple Inc.'s Customer Service Helpline

Apple Inc.'s customer service helpline

(Source: Adapted from www.apple.com/uk/, 2007)

Figure 5: Apple Inc.'s Customer Support Section

(Source: Adapted from www.apple.com/uk/, 2007)

2.1.5 Industry Restructuring

According to Chaffey *et al.* (2003) "disintermediation and reintermediation are key concepts of industry restructuring" (p.32) as new networking systems for managing the supply and value chain can be developed. As the business environment virtually and physically gets more intense and dynamic, information exchange and efficiency improvements are vital in order to sustain competitive and, more crucially lower costs while, according to Sheth and Sharma (2005), "the primary advantage of e-marketing is reducing costs and enhancing reach" (p.612) to supplier, retailers and customers. Bypassing existing channels of distribution is particularly important for a channel management in order to deliver value to the customers, such as free delivery from efficient distribution management. Thus, the Internet becomes very important in considering a company's representation of intermediaries (Chaffey *et al.*, 2003).

2.1.6 Independence of Location

According to Sheth and Sharma (2005), the e-marketing approach allows reaching customer, independent of location, to be accessible which might not be possible without applying this technology. The Internet makes it possible to enter international markets without being

8

physically present in those markets due to the delivery of digitalised products, e.g. music downloads (Figure 6), music player (Figure 7) or software updates (Figure 8).

Figure 6: Apple Inc.'s iTunes Music Download

(Source: Adapted from www.apple.com/uk/, 2007)

Figure 7: Apple Inc.'s iTunes Music Player Download

(Source: Adapted from www.apple.com/uk/, 2007)

9

Figure 8: Apple Inc.'s Software Updates

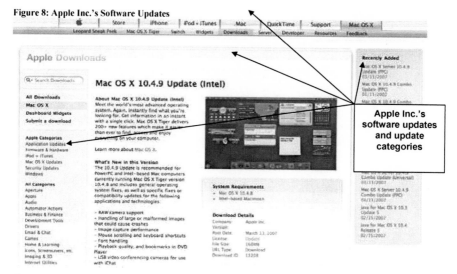

(Source: Adapted from www.apple.com/uk/, 2007)

However, there are existing challenges and disadvantages whilst enabling these technologies. In particular, they do not necessarily change "the elements and challenges associated with international marketing processes" but does change the nature and scope of international marketing strategies and "the solutions that are developed" (Doole and Lowe, 2004, p.404).

2.2 Threats & Challenges of Enabling Technologies

According to Sultan and Rohn (2004), cited in Tiago *et al.* (2007), "a few years back, enterprises questioned the role of the Internet in business performance, but today they cannot live without it, or outside it" (p.138). Nevertheless, although the Internet provides major advantages in international marketing and business operations, it still encounters disadvantages and its application can be a vast challenge for marketers. International e-businesses are facing challenges regarding the cultural background of the customers, as according to Doole and Lowe (2004), customers in "low context cultures are likely to embrace the Internet much more readily than those in high context cultures" (p.424). In addition, the Internet marketing strategy shall integrate all aspects of the traditional marketing strategy in order to deliver a unified and conformed picture of their marketing

10

communications and brand values. Otherwise, despite the undoubted potential of e-marketing, the whole marketing approach will not meet customers' expectations. Global Internet strategies should consider different infrastructural developments and environments that are existent in several countries and lengthy web site loading procedures might put customers off, especially those without broadband connections. Poor web site performance or design and slow order fulfilment can alienate customers from doing business with an organisation (Doole and Lowe, 2004). Therefore, a company has to set the focal point on providing adequate and reliable services for their customers throughout the whole online experience. As an increasing number of organisations are virtually present combined with proactive user behaviour, businesses have to ensure targeting the right audience with their communications campaign, virtually and physically, in order to overcome the Internet clutter. Adding value online is a prerequisite for companies to enable customers to experience something they cannot encounter offline. Due to this fact, organisations have to ensure they provide this value, otherwise the online presence will not stand out in the crowd. Furthermore, most online purchases require credit card information and thus "it is in the supplier's (and customer's) interest that the transaction is as safe and secure as possible", according to Molenaar (2002, p.71), in order not to dissatisfy the purchaser. Another conflict that might occur while applying the Internet purely as a sales medium is that some buyers need an incentive to purchase online, e.g. Apple Inc.'s online discount (Figure 9). Businesses which simply copy their physical product range to their web site might force a buying conflict in which the customer does not know why he/she should buy online and so do not meet the needs and wants of the customer (Molenaar, 2002).

Figure 9: Apple Inc.'s Online Discount Incentives

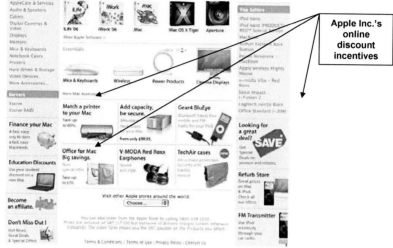

Apple Inc.'s online discount incentives

(Source: Adapted from www.apple.com/uk/, 2007)

As technology is rapidly developing and constantly changing, businesses must respond to technological changes in order to retain and develop customers. The model of the vicious circle of technology and competitive advantage (Figure 10) identifies that technology adds no value until it has practical applications for the user (Doole and Lowe, 2004). Technological knowledge and skills are prerequisites for implementing and adapting new technologies to business operations and once a new technology is invented and applied, another might already exist to supersede the previous one. Therefore it can be argued that technology, if implemented successfully, will result in competitive advantage by virtue of an ever changing and dynamic infinite loop until technology stops, if it ever will.

Figure 10: The Vicious Circle of Technology & Competitive Advantage

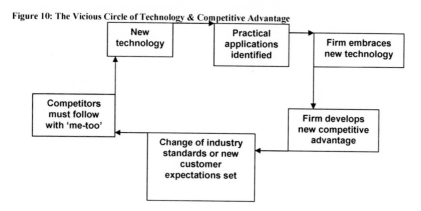

(Source: Adapted from Doole and Lowe, 2004, International Marketing Strategy, 4th edition. London, Thomson Learning)

3. Internet Marketing Strategy

The increasing pressures of using new media formats impact on businesses as they have to cope with new competitors, such as pure play companies, and therefore need to adapt and integrate their offline marketing objectives, strategies and tactics to their online marketing activities. According to Kotler (2001), cited in Chaffey *et al.* (2003), "the key question is not whether to deploy Internet technology – companies have no choice if they want to stay competitive – but how to deploy it" (p.134). As the Internet marketing strategy provides a long-term direction for the company's e-marketing activity, they have to bear in mind that "the potential will hardly be achieved unless the objectives are clearly defined and integrated into the company strategy" (Tiago *et al.*, 2007, p.139). Although Internet marketing strategy approaches have several similarities to the traditional marketing strategy, it still requires a different method, as the environment is fundamentally diverse (Eid and Trueman, 2002). The initial stage of an Internet marketing strategy development is the definition and setting of objectives, because the e-marketing strategy, in order to be effective, according to Mohammed (2003), "needs to be consistent with the firm's business strategy" (p.88) and furthermore, must be "highly aligned" (p.88) and synchronised with the business strategy, as well as deduced from the business mission. By enabling technologies, the marketplace, the macro- and micro-environmental assessment of organisations can be eased and isochronously become more transparent. According to Doole and Lowe (2004), "firms can track political,

13

economic and legal changes and new product launches by competitors" (p.420), which provide e-marketing organisations with an up-to-date analysis. Thus, as technology-enabling companies have to be aware of the dynamic environment they are operating in, tactical adaptation, such as pricing, can be implemented with increased speed. As Apple Inc. delivers new products and technological innovations to the marketplace, their e-marketing segmentation, targeting and positioning strategies differ from traditional marketing approaches in terms of a finer segmentation because customer behaviour can be tracked faster, be easier understood and thus, more adequately identified (Mohammed, 2003) and finally targeted. For example Apple Inc. simplified their computer product segmentation (Figure 11) in comparison to their pre-online presence (Figure 12), as illustrated in the following.

Figure 11: Apple Inc.'s Computer Product Segmentation 2007

	Desktop Computer	Portable Computer
Consumer usage	iMac, MacMini	MacBook
Professional usage	Mac Pro	MacBook Pro

(Source: Adapted from http://its.syr.edu/web/, 2007)

Figure 12: Apple Inc.'s Computer Product Segmentation 1997

Desktop Computer	Portable Computer
PowerMac 9600	PowerBook 2400
PowerMac 8600	PowerBook 3400
PowerMac 7300	PowerBook G3
PowerMac 6500	
PowerMac G3	

(Source: Adapted from http://its.syr.edu/web/, 2007)

Hence, marketing strategies can be faster adapted and updated through the increased speed of information-gathering processes from applying technology, however "the implementation of e-marketing strategies in international markets adds an increased level of complexity" (Sheth and Sharma, 2005, p.612), e.g. adapting the online presence to the individual target country's infrastructure. Although Apple Inc. uses the same online approach in all targeted countries, country specific adaptations are existent, e.g. content and layout (Figure 13).

Figure 13: Comparison Between Apple Inc.'s Web Site in the UK & Iceland (Customer Support Section)

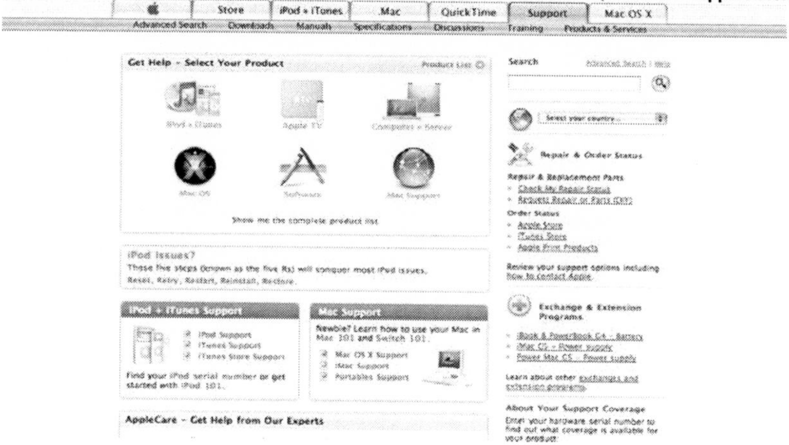

(Source: Adapted from www.apple.com/uk/, 2007)

(Source: Adapted from www.apple.is/, 2007)

3.1 Online Competitive Advantage

To achieve competitive advantage and customer orientation, three key elements (Figure 14) must be met by an organisation, according to Tracy and Wiersema (1994), cited in Molenaar (2002).

Figure 14: Competitive Advantage & Customer Orientation

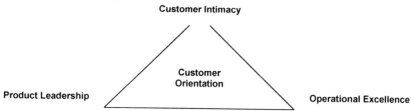

(Source: Adapted from Molenaar, Cor (2002) *The Future of Marketing – Practical Strategies for Marketers in the Post-Internet Age*. Harlow, Prentice Hall.)

This model can be linked to Rajshekhar's *et al.* (2005) model of gaining sustainable competitive advantage on the Internet, as three key components, namely the consumer decision-making process, the CRM and the firm's performance influence the development of online competitive advantage. It can be argued that Apple Inc. has gained a sustainable product leadership advantage through their innovative designs and superiority of their products combined with customer-centric applications. Furthermore, Apple Inc.'s corporate brand identity is of crucial importance for customers and their intimacy, because trust and satisfaction are important parts of gaining a close relationship to Apple Inc., as "Apple is among the high-technology companies with the most loyal customers" (MacNN, 2006) which can be related to their operational excellence, and vice versa. Apple Inc. has also gained a sustainable operational excellence advantage through their strategic partnerships and relationship approaches while enabling technology, e.g. Apple Inc. established a relationship with the Adobe Company in order to provide their customers with current software applications that are available on their web site that underlines their virtual partnership advantage (Figure 15). In addition, Apple Inc.'s partnership with Nike identifies a competitive advantage of innovative products in order to enhance customer experience through design, connectivity and product superiority (Figure 16).

16

Figure 15: Apple Inc.'s & Adobe Company's Online Relationship

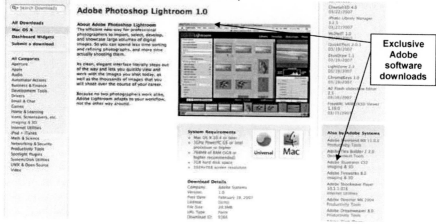

(Source: Adapted from www.apple.com/uk/, 2007)

Figure 16: Apple Inc.'s & Nike's Product Relationship

(Source: Adapted from www.apple.com/uk/, 2007)

Another example can be acknowledged from Apple Inc.'s podcast technology that bonds customers to the web site by offering a variety of interactive and integrative tools for Apple Inc.'s iPod products (Figure 17).

Figure 17: Apple Inc.'s Podcast Download Technology

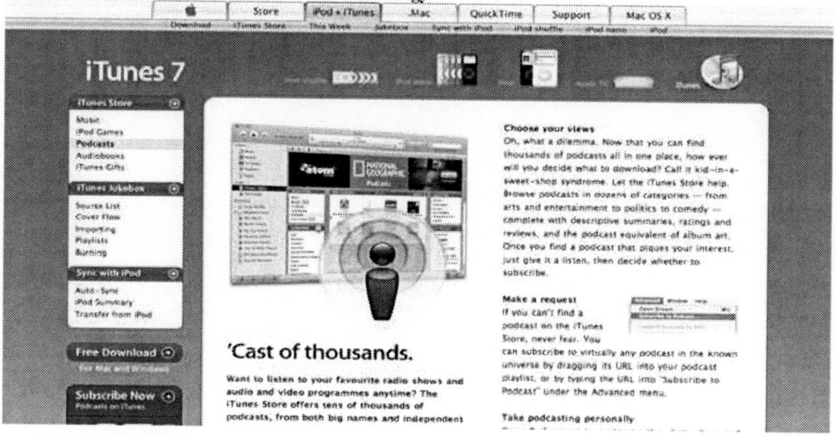

(Source: Adapted from www.apple.com/uk/, 2007)

Affiliation programme strategies "seek to create customer trust on the web and encourage web site visits" (Verona and Prandelli, 2002, cited in Rajshekhar *et al.*, 2005, p.663). Apple Inc. created an affiliation programme in order to let the customer participate in the cooperation, e.g. iTunes affiliates (Figure 18) or even in NPD development through Apple Inc.'s Developer Connection (Figure 19), to strengthen loyalty, brand preferences and allow customers to be involved as evangelists, e.g. discussion, chats and forums, in a customer relationship approach.

Figure 18: Apple Inc.'s iTunes Affiliation Programme

(Source: Adapted from www.apple.com/uk/, 2007)

Figure 19: Apple Inc.'s Developer Connection Programme

(Source: Adapted from www.apple.com/uk/, 2007)

Furthermore, in order to sustain competitive advantage, customer's decision-making stages are linked to the web site navigation (Rajshekhar, 2005). Apple Inc. applies a consistent web

19

site design combined with an easy-to-use layout, which supports customers' decision-making processes in finding what they are searching for.

Apple Inc.'s strategic approach focuses on the online value proposition related to their core proposition of delivering the best personal computing technology to their various target audiences on- and offline. Therefore it can be argued, that Apple Inc. has developed a product leadership approach combined with operational excellence and customer intimacy, as their services and products set the focal point on innovative usage, customer-focused applications, excellent services and design, which therefore highlights the customer orientation of the company and the development of competitive advantages online. The better the customer experiences are on the web site in all aspects, the more likely are they in returning and purchasing again.

3.2. The E-marketing Mix

The marketing mix on the Internet differs, in terms of the process, from the traditional marketing mix, as according to (Eid and Trueman, 2002) the "marketing effort on the Internet will be an interactive strategy" (p.55).

3.2.1 Product

The product element of the marketing mix refers, according to Chaffey *et al.* (2003) "to characteristics of a product, service or brand" (p.184). As the Internet "presents companies with unique opportunities to enhance their product offerings" (Mohammed *et al.*, 2003, p.241), product characteristics can be divided into four distinct categories.

3.2.1.1 Digitalised Goods

By enabling technologies certain goods can be delivered in a digitalised format, e.g. Apple Inc.'s software, updates, music downloads or podcasts, which provides an augmented benefit to the user, along with envisaged problems as the ease of duplication is existent. Digitalised products can be easily tailored by the customer and for the customer in order to meet the customers' individual needs and wants, such as Apple Inc.'s "My Account" feature.

3.2.1.2 Service

Services can provide augmented value to the product in terms of interacting with customers. Apple Inc. offers online help services or support sections where the customer can search for answers to particular problems without human interaction, i.e. the seller and buyer of a service need not be in the same place at the same time (Mohammed *et al.*, 2003). Furthermore, services can also be tailored to the personal needs of a customer and thus provide a basis for customisation and interactivity.

3.2.1.3 Product Augmentation

The Internet has offered the chance of product augmentations and new product developments, e.g. Apple Inc.'s Developer Connection, while related online products, such as updates, podcasts or increased service offers can be purchased. This would not be available without applying this medium. In addition, the Internet provides services for pre- and post-purchase support programmes, such as purchase recommendations or feedback questionnaires, in order to enhance customer value and trust.

3.2.1.4 Product Assortment

The Internet, according to Mohammed *et al.* (2003) "has led to an increase in the number of product variants offered" (p.248), in order to get the customer to the web site, e.g. special offers or bundling opportunities which are exclusively available online. Complementary products, e.g. iTunes gift vouchers, can be approximated to the customer and once again offer the chance to personalise products for the customer and integrate on- and offline media.

However, the product related mix also faces a challenge with regards to a decreasing product-life-cycle span, due to rapid innovations in technology (see also 'the vicious circle of technology and competitive advantage'). As technology evolves, product changes and adaptation have to be executed with an increased momentum in which some companies might find problems with.

3.2.2 Place

According to Wilson and Abel (2002), cited in Eid and Trueman (2002), "the Internet is borderless and the opportunity to sell over the net eliminates many natural barriers to entry" (p.58). Due to the fact that Internet companies are able to sell their good nearly anywhere in the world, while, in parallel, reduces traditional intermediaries in international trade.

According to Mohammed *et al.* (2003), this facilitates collaborative relationships due to more efficient channel management and furthermore connects the "end-user and producer directly" (Eid and Trueman, 2002, p.58), e.g. Apple Inc. offers the customer the choice to identify and track where the dispatched product is currently situated while being shipped to the customer (Figure 20). Disintermediation eliminates the middlemen and companies can profit from economies of scales and cost efficiency, and vice versa.

Figure 20: Apple Inc.'s "Track Your Order" Feature

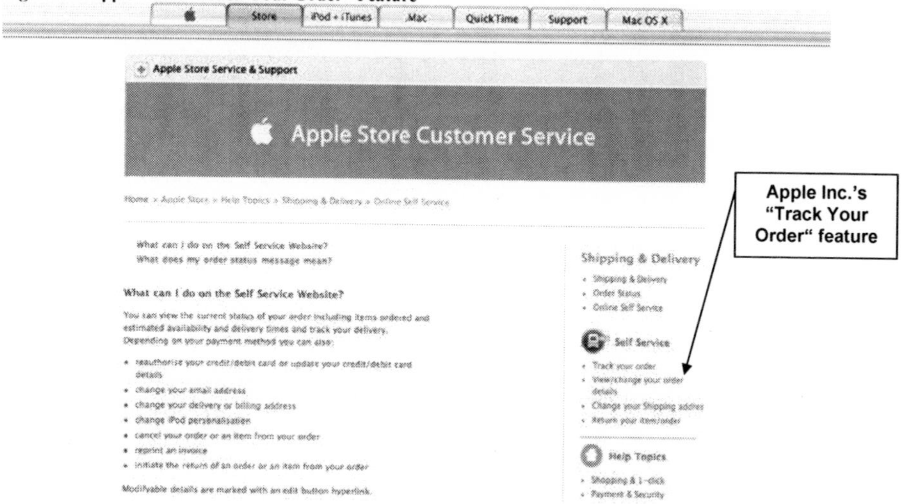

(Source: Adapted from www.apple.com/uk/, 2007)

Companies that maintain intermediaries within their channel distribution management can gain much closer collaborations with their intermediaries and, furthermore, are able to exchange market information (Doole and Lowe, 2004) in order to improve the channel efficiency.

3.2.3 Promotion

The main advantages of e-marketing communications are "that they are targeted and are often based on one-to-one communications" (Doole and Lowe, 2004, p.423) which is essential in a customer-centric marketing strategy. The Internet provides new and innovative possibilities of executing an integrated marketing communications campaign, as targeting can be performed

more accurately due to the precise placement of online media promotional tools, such as banner ads (Figure 21), interstitials, dynamic ad placement or opt-in email.

Figure 21: Apple Inc.'s Banner Advertisement on Product Related Web Sites

(Source: Adapted from www.macnn.com/, 2007)

The Internet facilitates the two-way communication relationship and allows a cost-efficient marketing communications evaluation methods (Mohammed *et al.*, 2003) and furthermore, it offers the chance to interrelate promotions by applying new communication approaches like m-marketing. Promotion wise, the Internet offers a creative basis for an interactive communication with the customer in order to enhance customers' online experiences. In addition, sending personalised newsletters to customers can customise the communication effort. The challenge however is "to be innovative and not replicate your conventional advertising material online" (Bickerton *et al.*, 2001, p.165) and integrates the offline with the online communication approach, and vice versa.

It can be argued that the e-marketing mix, by enabling the Internet, requires a completely different approach in executing the whole marketing mix programme, as the environment for international marketing is fundamentally different (Eid and Trueman, 2002) and the entire tactical approach is decisively dissimilar from traditional marketing mix.

3.3. The Internet & Pricing

With respect to pricing, the Internet provides "both new threats and opportunities for companies" (Karlsson *et al.*, 2005, p.351) in comparison to offline pricing approaches. Due to its dynamism, the Internet has an influence on the strategic pricing decisions (Eid and Trueman, 2002) as it is more cost efficient to implement dynamic pricing strategies. The Internet offers users various advantages in terms of comparing prices (Bickerton *et al.*, 2001) as the transparency of this medium contributes an easement regarding the search for a low price from alternative sellers. But "as easy it is for a price conscious customer to find the lowest price, the Internet increases the chances for the firms to find a buyer willing to pay a higher price" (Kung *et al.*, 2002, p.280). Furthermore, searching online for products can be convenient and comparatively cheap, as expenditure to process information, such as driving, negotiation or telephone calls will be crucially decreased in comparison to traditional shopping (Karlsson *et al.*, 2005). But to make an accurate price comparison "online consumer must have available not only the price of the product but also the shipping fees, sales tax, and other offer/transaction information" (Kung *et al.*, 2002, p.278) which adds complexity to the whole buying process in terms of comparing offers on various web sites for a certain product or service.

Nevertheless, the Internet enable companies to understand and measure customers' reactions to price promotions and eases the process of tracking that information in order to adjust prices to customers' willingness to pay (Mohammed *et al.*, 2003), e.g. Apple's business customer vs. students. According to Chaffey *et al.* (2003) and Karlsson *et al.* (2005), the Internet tends to drive down prices due to disintermediation and commoditisation, and leads to a state of a perfect market, on the basis of the greater number of competitors present combined with an increased visibility of prices. But one of the Internet's advantages is the individualisation aspect of products, prices or promotions, which is contradictory to a perfect homogeneous market structure. The better a brand is individually differentiated from competitive brands, the more less is will be a subject to drive down the price as brand loyalty offers the chance to increase prices. Furthermore, the Internet enables companies to categorise and understand each customer segment, which facilitates organisations ability to provide segment-specific prices (Kung *et al.*, 2002). By enabling technology, several cost efficient opportunities can be identified due to alternative online price approaches. According to Chaffey *et al.* (2003) "the Internet introduces new opportunities for dynamic pricing" (p.199) in which prices "are fluid"

(Mohammed *et al.*, 2003, p.295), i.e. dynamically changing due to environmental influences. "The Internet enhances the attractiveness of the dynamic pricing strategy" (Mohammed *et al.*, 2003, p.295) in two key directions, as decreased menu cost result from applying this strategy and furthermore, the ability to negotiate prices in real time online. Dynamic pricing offers the opportunity to change prices rapidly in comparison to offline pricing methods, as companies can instantly adjust online prices due to demand and supply situations. As the Internet provides an important element "in the paradigm shift that will profoundly alter the way goods are marketed and sold" (Kung *et al.*, 2002, p.280), it will also lead to the ability of segmenting and tracking customers in an increasingly efficient and effective way. In addition, the Internet enables companies to offer tailored offers to individual customer segments, e.g. Apple Inc.'s tailored offers for schools (Figure 22) and universities (Figure 23).

Figure 22: Apple Inc.'s Special Deals for Schools

(Source: Adapted from www.apple.com/uk/, 2007)

Figure 23: Apple Inc.'s Special Deals For Universities

Apple Inc.'s
special deals
for universities

(Source: Adapted from www.apple.com/uk/, 2007)

Other pricing strategies from enabling technology can be identified as advanced pricing strategies, including tactical offers such as bundling or volume discount pricing (Mohammed et al., 2003). Apple Inc. offers its customer special prices when ordering a certain volume of products, e.g. iPods, which are exclusively available online (Figure 24).

Figure 24: Apple Inc.'s Special Volume Discount Offers (iPod)

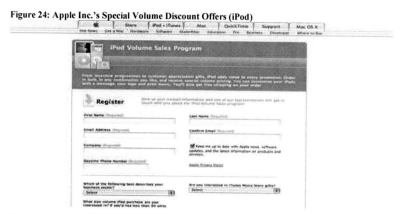

(Source: Adapted from www.apple.com/uk/, 2007)

In order to increase Internet purchases, companies can provide certain bundles in order to differentiate itself from other organisations or even price comparison web site services, as those bundles can be solely purchased online, e.g. Apple Inc.'s MacBook and printer bundle (Figure 25).

Figure 25: Apple Inc.'s MacBook & Printer Bundle

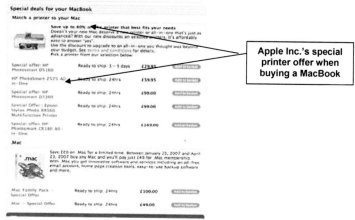

(Source: Adapted from www.apple.com/uk/, 2007)

By applying the above-mentioned pricing strategies via the Internet, businesses can monitor and test prices, "discover new segments and continuously change prices based on customer preferences" (Kung *et al.*, 2002, p.280).

However, Kung *et al.*, (2002) argue that customers return and purchase on particular web sites with which they had good experiences and are familiar with, due to for instance, security concerns, a superiority of service or the availability of adequate information. According to this research, this leads to an increase in online customer loyalty and offers businesses the chance to increase their prices, as they have developed a competitive advantage from their corporate brand identity and brand loyal customers, and vice versa. Lynch and Ariely (2002), cited in Kung *et al.* (2002), argue that, "consumers become less price sensitive and more loyal as the level of quality information on a site increases" (p.277) which may be a possible indicator that the Internet does not necessarily drive down prices, as brand loyalty for certain web sites and products increase.

Nevertheless, businesses have to be aware of possible grey marketing facilitations, if they differentiate their prices geographically too rigorous (Doole and Lowe, 2004).

4. Critical Evaluation of Apple Inc.'s Web Site

In order to provide a critical evaluation of Apple Inc.'s web site strengths and weaknesses, combined with proposed improvements of the web site will be examined according to the above-analysed insights regarding cybermarketing issues.

4.1 Strengths

Apple Inc.'s web site is globally consistent in terms of layout design and navigation experiences. According to Taylor and England (2006), organisations have to ensure that "their web site is straightforward and appealing to use" (p.77) in order to attract and retain customers. Apple Inc.'s web site is designed to appeal to the customer by providing a tab and sub navigation menu, as well as a product menu at the left hand side (Figure 26), which eases navigation. Furthermore, Apple Inc. provides dynamic features, e.g. watching current TV ads, and therefore allows customers to experience the web site interactively (Figure 27).

Figure 26: Apple Inc.'s Web Site Navigation

(Source: Adapted from www.apple.com/uk/, 2007)

Figure 27: Apple Inc.'s Interactivity Feature (TV Ads)

(Source: Adapted from www.apple.com/uk/, 2007)

Using white spaces on their web site can create a "sense of clam" (Mohammed et al., 2003, p.163) and draws the user's attention to Apple Inc.'s products (Figure 28). Adequate information contents and menu categories are implemented in a straightforward and simplified way in order to ease the searching procedure for the user. Individualisation issues such as "My Account" and participation and affiliation programmes, i.e. being involved in NPD or taking exclusive part in special Apple Inc. events levers evangelistic customer experiences. Furthermore, Apple Inc. segments their web site for different target audiences and adjust the content to their specific needs and wants (Figure 29 & Figure 30) which underlines Apple Inc.'s customer-centric online approach. Another strength of this web site is the immediate visible call-of-action feature, which eases users the purchasing of their products (Figure 31). To conclude, it can be said that this organisation understands their online approach, while providing individualisation and interactivity for users. It can be also argued that this is due to the nature of Apple Inc.'s business.

Figure 28: Apple Inc.'s Web Site Layout

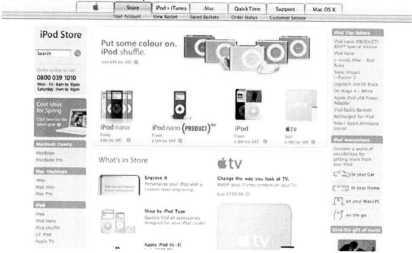

(Source: Adapted from www.apple.com/uk/, 2007)

Figure 29: Apple Inc.'s Specific Target Audience Layout (Students)

(Source: Adapted from www.apple.com/uk/, 2007)

Figure 30: Apple Inc.'s Specific Target Audience Layout (Businesses)

(Source: Adapted from www.apple.com/uk/, 2007)

Figure 31: Apple Inc.'s Call-of-Action Feature (iPod)

Call-of-action feature

(Source: Adapted from www.apple.com/uk/, 2007)

4.2 Weaknesses & Proposed Improvements

However, despite the strengths of Apple Inc.'s web site, there are also weaknesses and areas of possible improvements in order to develop the web site even further. Besides the "My Account" section, which focuses on purchases and related products, Apple Inc. could provide a member login section for specific tailored information about the company, events and future products. This could be used in order to collect customer data and thus, develop a specialised database in order to target certain customer with even more precision whilst enhancing Apple Inc.'s web presence. Another major weakness is that some content of their web site provides extensively overwhelming features which makes it difficult for the user, especially for those which have not extensively used complex web sites, to navigate and search for information (Figure 32). These are the major identified weaknesses, which could be improved to make this web site even better.

Figure 32: Apple Inc.'s Complex Web Site Content

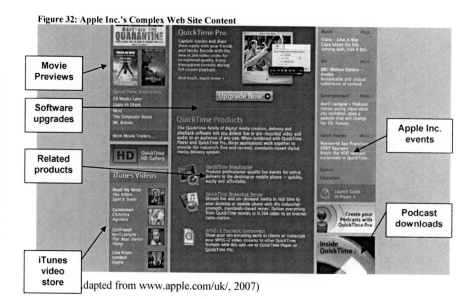

(Adapted from www.apple.com/uk/, 2007)

5. Conclusion

This report has critically analysed the effects that enabling technologies are having on the marketing strategy of businesses. Focusing on the Apple Inc., in order to provide a basis on

which to illustrate and underline major cybermarketing aspects. Enabling technologies provide businesses with the chance to operate globally and furthermore, offer the opportunity to provide services to customers that they would not be able to without applying technology. Although technology provides organisations with profound advantages and opportunities, parallel to this are the vast challenges and threats as the number of competitors in the marketspace increase, combined with the constant innovation of technologies. Thus, e-marketers must constantly be able to adapt new technologies to their organisation in order to provide value to their existing and potential customers and stakeholders. The companies, which implement the newest technology, and thus allocate a practical value for the user, will be ahead of the competition, but maybe not for a long time, due to dynamic technological improvements. As e-marketing provides the chance to establish a two-way communication loop with customers and stakeholder and, in addition, offers the possibility to interactively individualise prices, promotions and products. From a sophisticated e-marketing mix, a competitive advantage may also result in implementing technologies.

By enabling technologies, a paradigm shift from traditional to new media strategy approaches can be identified that highlights increased feasibility in executing global online marketing strategies. This, however, also increases pressures due to globalisation and new competitive environments. Technological skills and knowledge are prerequisites in implementing a successful e-marketing campaign, but nevertheless, due to technological innovations, opportunities to gain advantages are vast as more and more people show affinity to technology nowadays. In today's rapid and dynamic environment, it is hardly possible to survive without enabling technology to a company, as it offers tremendous possibilities for businesses, if deployed in the appropriate way.

Managers must be able to cope with the challenges in order to harvest opportunities from enabling technologies, since technology might or might not be an infinite loop of innovation.

6. References

- Apple Inc. (2007) *Adobe Company Software Downloads* [Internet]. Apple Inc. Online. Available from: http://www.apple.com/downloads/macosx/internet_utilities/adobereader.html [Accessed 25th March 2007].

- Apple Inc. (2007) *Apple Inc. Account* [Internet]. Apple Inc. Online. Available from: http://submit.macsoftware.apple.com/uscontact/addFeedback.lasso [Accessed 20th March 2007].

- Apple Inc. (2007) *Apple Inc. Customer Support* [Internet]. Apple Inc. Online. Available from: http://www.apple.com/uk/support/ [Accessed 19th March 2007].

- Apple Inc. (2007) *Apple Inc. Developer Connection Programme* [Internet]. Apple Inc. Online. Available from: http://developer.apple.com/ [Accessed 25th March 2007].

- Apple Inc. (2007) *Apple Inc. Education - Schools* [Internet]. Apple Inc. Online. Available from: http://www.apple.com/uk/education/schools/ [Accessed 26th March 2007].

- Apple Inc. (2007) *Apple Inc. Special Volume Discount* [Internet]. Apple Inc. Online. Available from: http://www.apple.com/uk/ipod/imaging/ [Accessed 24th March 2007].

- Apple Inc. (2007) *Apple Inc. Education - Students* [Internet]. Apple Inc. Online. Available from: http://www.apple.com/uk/education/hed/students/ [Accessed 22nd March 2007].

- Apple Inc. (2007) *Apple Inc. Education - Universities* [Internet]. Apple Inc. Online. Available from: http://www.apple.com/uk/education/hed/ [Accessed 26th March 2007].

- Apple Inc. (2007) *Apple Inc. Iceland Customer Support* [Internet]. Apple Inc. Online. Available from: http://www.apple.is/thjonusta/ [Accessed 24th March 2007].

- Apple Inc. (2007) *Apple Inc. iTunes Affiliates* [Internet]. Apple Inc. Online. Available from: http://www.apple.com/uk/itunes/affiliates/ [Accessed 24th March 2007].

- Apple Inc. (2007) *Apple Inc. iTunes Music Player Download* [Internet]. Apple Inc. Online. Available from: http://www.apple.com/uk/itunes/download/ [Accessed 20th March 2007].

- Apple Inc. (2007) *Apple Inc. iTunes Music Store* [Internet]. Apple Inc. Online. Available from: http://www.apple.com/uk/itunes/store/ [Accessed 21st March 2007].

- Apple Inc. (2007) *Macintosh Products Guide - Feedback* [Internet]. Apple Inc. Online. Available from: http://submit.macsoftware.apple.com/uscontact/addFeedback.lasso [Accessed 20th March 2007].

- Apple Inc. (2007) *Apple Inc. & Nike Products* [Internet]. Apple Inc. Online. Available from: http://www.apple.com/uk/ipod/nike/ [Accessed 25th March 2007].

- Apple Inc. (2007) *Apple Inc. Order Status* [Internet]. Apple Inc. Online. Available from: https://store.apple.com/Apple/WebObjects/OrderStatusUK?mid=appleukglobal%2Cap plestoreWW%2CapplestoreEMEA%2CapplestoreEMEAUK%2CapplestoreEMEAcon sum%2CapplestoreEMEAUKconsum&appleStoreSessionKey=992oYKn1fm8d3s3w QgC2NmlsxYV561921&csname=uk [Accessed 23rd March 2007].

- Apple Inc. (2007) *Apple Inc. Podcast Download* [Internet]. Apple Inc. Online. Available from: http://www.apple.com/uk/itunes/store/podcasts.html [Accessed 26th March 2007].

- Apple Inc. (2007) *Apple Inc. Quick Time Player* [Internet]. Apple Inc. Online. Available from: http://www.apple.com/uk/quicktime/mac.html [Accessed 25th March 2007].

- Apple Inc. (2007) *Apple Inc. Software Download* [Internet]. Apple Inc. Online. Available from: http://www.apple.com/uk/downloads/macosx/ [Accessed 20th March 2007].

- Apple Inc. (2007) *Apple Inc. Store* [Internet]. Apple Inc. Online. Available from: http://store.apple.com/Apple/WebObjects/ukstore [Accessed 19th March 2007].

- Bickerton, Pauline *et al.* (2001) *Cybermarketing – How to Use the Internet to Market Our Goods and Services*, 2nd edition. Oxford, Butterworth-Heinemann.

- Chaffey, Dave *et al.* (2003) *Internet Marketing – Strategy, Implementation and Practice*, 2nd edition. Harlow, Prentice Hall.

- Creativeclub (2007) *Apple Inc.'s iPod Print Advertisement* [Internet]. Creativeclub Online. Available from: http://www.creativeclub.co.uk/(k24lhmzxto2ecy4531c0wp45)/fs.aspx [Accessed 21st March 2007].

- Doole, Isobel and Lowe, Robin (2004) *International Marketing Strategy – Analysis, Development and Implementation*, 4th edition. London, Thomson Learning.

- Eid, Riyad and Trueman, Myfanwy (2002) The Internet: New International Marketing Issues. *Management Research News*, 25(12), p.54-67. Available from: http://www.emeraldinsight.com/Insight/ViewContentServlet?Filename=Published/EmeraldAbstractOnlyArticle/Articles/0210251203.html [Accessed 21st March 2007].

- Internet World Stats (2007) *Global Internet Usage Statistics* [Internet]. Internet World Stats Online. Available from: http://www.internetworldstats.com/stats.htm [Accessed 20th March 2007].

- Internet World Stats (2007) *Internet Usage in Europe* [Internet]. Internet World Stats Online. Available from: http://www.internetworldstats.com/stats4.htm [Accessed 20th March 2007].

- Karlsson, Ted *et al.* (2005) Prices as a Variable in Online Consumer Trade-offs. *Marketing Intelligence & Planning*, 23(4), p.350-358. Available from: http://www.emeraldinsight.com/Insight/ViewContentServlet?Filename=Published/EmeraldFullTextArticle/Articles/0200230402.html [Accessed 23rd March 2007].

- Kung, Mui *et al.* (2002) Pricing on the Internet. *Journal of Product & Brand Management*, 11(5), p.274-287. Available from: http://www.emeraldinsight.com/Insight/ViewContentServlet?Filename=Published/EmeraldFullTextArticle/Articles/0960110501.html [Accessed 24th March 2007].

- MacNN (2007) *Apple, Google tops in loyalty survey* [Internet]. MacNN Online. Available from: http://www.macnn.com/articles/06/07/11/apple.google.find.loyalty/ [Accessed 22nd March 2007].

- MacNN (2007) *Apple Inc.'s Banner Advertisement* [Internet]. MacNN Online. Available from: http://www.macnn.com/ [Accessed 22nd March 2007].

- Mohammed, Rafi *et al.* (2003) *Internet Marketing – Building Advantage in a Networked Economy*, 2nd edition. London, McGraw-Hill.

- Molenaar, Cor (2002) *The Future of Marketing – Practical Strategies for Marketers in the Internet Age*. Harlow, Prentice Hall.

- Rajshekhar, Javalgi *et al.* (2005) Sustainable Competitive Advantage of Internet Firms: A Strategic Framework and Implications for Global Marketers. *International Marketing Review*, 22(6), p.658-672. Available from: http://www.emeraldinsight.com/Insight/ViewContentServlet?Filename=Published/Em eraldFullTextArticle/Articles/0360220605.html [Accessed 21st March 2007].

- Sheth, Jagdish and Sharma, Arun (2005) International e-Marketing: Opportunities and Issues. *International Marketing Review*, 22(6), p.611-622. Available from: http://proquest.umi.com/pqdweb?index=0&did=956680571&SrchMode=1&sid=2&F mt=4&VInst=PROD&VType=PQD&RQT=309&VName=PQD&TS=1175191664&cl ientId=57096 [Accessed 23rd March 2007].

- Syracuse University (2007) *Apple Inc.'s Computer Product Segmentation* [Internet]. Syracuse University Online. Available from: http://its.syr.edu/web/ [Accessed 23rd March 2007].

- Taylor, M.J. and England, D. (2006) Internet Marketing: Web Site Navigational Design Issues. *Marketing Intelligence & Planning*, 24(1), p.77-85. Available from: http://www.emeraldinsight.com/Insight/ViewContentServlet?Filename=Published/Em eraldFullTextArticle/Articles/0200240106.html [Accessed 20th March 2007].

- Tiago, Maria *et al.* (2007) International Reality of Internet Use as Marketing Tool. *Journal of American Academy of Business*, 11(1), p.138-144. Available from: http://proquest.umi.com/pqdweb?index=0&did=1186428261&SrchMode=1&sid=1&F mt=4&VInst=PROD&VType=PQD&RQT=309&VName=PQD&TS=1175191275&cl ientId=57096 [Accessed 20th March 2007].

7. Bibliographies

- Apple Inc. (2007) *Adobe Company Software Downloads* [Internet]. Apple Inc. Online. Available from: http://www.apple.com/downloads/macosx/internet_utilities/adobereader.html [Accessed 25th March 2007].

- Apple Inc. (2007) *Apple Inc. Account* [Internet]. Apple Inc. Online. Available from:

http://submit.macsoftware.apple.com/uscontact/addFeedback.lasso   [Accessed   20th March 2007].

- Apple Inc. (2007) *Apple Inc. Customer Support* [Internet]. Apple Inc. Online. Available from:
  http://www.apple.com/uk/support/ [Accessed 19th March 2007].
- Apple Inc. (2007) *Apple Inc. Developer Connection Programme* [Internet]. Apple Inc. Online. Available from:
  http://developer.apple.com/ [Accessed 25th March 2007].
- Apple Inc. (2007) *Apple Inc. Education - Schools* [Internet]. Apple Inc. Online. Available from:
  http://www.apple.com/uk/education/schools/ [Accessed 26th March 2007].
- Apple Inc. (2007) *Apple Inc. Special Volume Discount* [Internet]. Apple Inc. Online. Available from:
  http://www.apple.com/uk/ipod/imaging/ [Accessed 24th March 2007].
- Apple Inc. (2007) *Apple Inc. Education - Students* [Internet]. Apple Inc. Online. Available from:
  http://www.apple.com/uk/education/hed/students/ [Accessed 22nd March 2007].
- Apple Inc. (2007) *Apple Inc. Education - Universities* [Internet]. Apple Inc. Online. Available from:
  http://www.apple.com/uk/education/hed/ [Accessed 26th March 2007].
- Apple Inc. (2007) *Apple Inc. Iceland Customer Support* [Internet]. Apple Inc. Online. Available from:
  http://www.apple.is/thjonusta/ [Accessed 24th March 2007].
- Apple Inc. (2007) *Apple Inc. iTunes Affiliates* [Internet]. Apple Inc. Online. Available from:
  http://www.apple.com/uk/itunes/affiliates/ [Accessed 24th March 2007].
- Apple Inc. (2007) *Apple Inc. iTunes Music Player Download* [Internet]. Apple Inc. Online. Available from:
  http://www.apple.com/uk/itunes/download/ [Accessed 20th March 2007].
- Apple Inc. (2007) *Apple Inc. iTunes Music Store* [Internet]. Apple Inc. Online. Available from:
  http://www.apple.com/uk/itunes/store/ [Accessed 21st March 2007].
- Apple Inc. (2007) *Macintosh Products Guide - Feedback* [Internet]. Apple Inc. Online. Available from:

http://submit.macsoftware.apple.com/uscontact/addFeedback.lasso   [Accessed   20th
March 2007].

- Apple Inc. (2007) *Apple Inc. & Nike Products* [Internet]. Apple Inc. Online. Available
  from:
  http://www.apple.com/uk/ipod/nike/ [Accessed 25th March 2007].

- Apple Inc. (2007) *Apple Inc. Order Status* [Internet]. Apple Inc. Online. Available
  from:
  https://store.apple.com/Apple/WebObjects/OrderStatusUK?mid=appleukglobal%2Cap
  plestoreWW%2CapplestoreEMEA%2CapplestoreEMEAUK%2CapplestoreEMEAcon
  sum%2CapplestoreEMEAUKconsum&appleStoreSessionKey=992oYKn1fm8d3s3w
  QgC2NmlsxYV561921&csname=uk [Accessed 23rd March 2007].

- Apple Inc. (2007) *Apple Inc. Podcast Download* [Internet]. Apple Inc. Online.
  Available from:
  http://www.apple.com/uk/itunes/store/podcasts.html [Accessed 26th March 2007].

- Apple Inc. (2007) *Apple Inc. Quick Time Player* [Internet]. Apple Inc. Online.
  Available from:
  http://www.apple.com/uk/quicktime/mac.html [Accessed 25th March 2007].

- Apple Inc. (2007) *Apple Inc. Software Download* [Internet]. Apple Inc. Online.
  Available from:
  http://www.apple.com/uk/downloads/macosx/ [Accessed 20th March 2007].

- Apple Inc. (2007) *Apple Inc. Store* [Internet]. Apple Inc. Online. Available from:
  http://store.apple.com/Apple/WebObjects/ukstore [Accessed 19th March 2007].

- Bickerton, Pauline *et al.* (2001) *Cybermarketing – How to Use the Internet to Market
  Our Goods and Services*, 2nd edition. Oxford, Butterworth-Heinemann.

- Chaffey, Dave *et al.* (2003) *Internet Marketing – Strategy, Implementation and
  Practice*, 2nd edition. Harlow, Prentice Hall.

- Creativeclub (2007) *Apple Inc.'s iPod Print Advertisement* [Internet]. Creativeclub
  Online. Available from:
  http://www.creativeclub.co.uk/(k24lhmzxto2ecy4531c0wp45)/fs.aspx [Accessed 21st
  March 2007].

- Doole, Isobel and Lowe, Robin (2004) *International Marketing Strategy – Analysis,
  Development and Implementation*, 4th edition. London, Thomson Learning.

- Eid, Riyad and Trueman, Myfanwy (2002) The Internet: New International Marketing
  Issues. *Management Research News*, 25(12), p.54-67. Available from:

http://www.emeraldinsight.com/Insight/ViewContentServlet?Filename=Published/EmeraldAbstractOnlyArticle/Articles/0210251203.html [Accessed 21st March 2007].

- Green, Andrew (2006) Can the Internet build a Brand?. *WARC Media FAQ*. Available from:

  http://www.warc.com/Search/WordSearch/Results.asp [Accessed 22nd March 2007].

- Hollensen, Svend (2004) *Global Marketing – A Decision-orientated Approach*, 3rd edition. Harlow, Prentice Hall.

- Internet World Stats (2007) *Global Internet Usage Statistics* [Internet]. Internet World Stats Online. Available from:

  http://www.internetworldstats.com/stats.htm [Accessed 20th March 2007].

- Internet World Stats (2007) *Internet Usage in Europe* [Internet]. Internet World Stats Online. Available from:

  http://www.internetworldstats.com/stats4.htm [Accessed 20th March 2007].

- Karlsson, Ted *et al.* (2005) Prices as a Variable in Online Consumer Trade-offs. *Marketing Intelligence & Planning*, 23(4), p.350-358. Available from:

  http://www.emeraldinsight.com/Insight/ViewContentServlet?Filename=Published/EmeraldFullTextArticle/Articles/0200230402.html [Accessed 23rd March 2007].

- Kung, Mui *et al.* (2002) Pricing on the Internet. *Journal of Product & Brand Management*, 11(5), p.274-287. Available from:

  http://www.emeraldinsight.com/Insight/ViewContentServlet?Filename=Published/EmeraldFullTextArticle/Articles/0960110501.html [Accessed 24th March 2007].

- MacNN (2007) *Apple, Google tops in loyalty survey* [Internet]. MacNN Online. Available from:

  http://www.macnn.com/articles/06/07/11/apple.google.find.loyalty/ [Accessed 22nd March 2007].

- MacNN (2007) *Apple Inc.'s Banner Advertisement* [Internet]. MacNN Online. Available from:

  http://www.macnn.com/ [Accessed 22nd March 2007].

- Mohammed, Rafi *et al.* (2003) *Internet Marketing – Building Advantage in a Networked Economy*, 2nd edition. London, McGraw-Hill.

- Molenaar, Cor (2002) *The Future of Marketing – Practical Strategies for Marketers in the Internet Age*. Harlow, Prentice Hall.

- Pickton, David and Broderick, Amanda (2005) *Integrated Marketing Communications*, 2nd edition. Harlow, Prentice Hall.

- Rajshekhar, Javalgi *et al.* (2005) Sustainable Competitive Advantage of Internet Firms: A Strategic Framework and Implications for Global Marketers. *International Marketing Review*, 22(6), p.658-672. Available from: http://www.emeraldinsight.com/Insight/ViewContentServlet?Filename=Published/Em eraldFullTextArticle/Articles/0360220605.html [Accessed 21st March 2007].

- Say, Mary and Oldfield, Simon (2003) The Importance of the Customer Experience. *Admap Magazine*, Issue 440, p.39-41. Available from: http://www.warc.com/Search/WordSearch/Results.asp [Accessed 19th March 2007].

- Schultz, Don (1998) Advertising into the next Millennium. *International Journal of Advertising*, 17(4). Available from: http://www.warc.com/Search/WordSearch/Results.asp [Accessed 20th March 2007].

- Sheth, Jagdish and Sharma, Arun (2005) International e-Marketing: Opportunities and Issues. *International Marketing Review*, 22(6), p.611-622. Available from: http://proquest.umi.com/pqdweb?index=0&did=956680571&SrchMode=1&sid=2&F mt=4&VInst=PROD&VType=PQD&RQT=309&VName=PQD&TS=1175191664&cl ientId=57096 [Accessed 23rd March 2007].

- Smith, PR and Chaffey, Dave (2002) *eMarketing excellence – The Heart of eBusiness,* Oxford, Butterworth-Heinemann.

- Keegan, Warren and Green, Mark (2005) *Global Marketing*, 4th edition. Harlow, Prentice Hall.

- Syracuse University (2007) *Apple Inc.'s Computer Product Segmentation* [Internet]. Syracuse University Online. Available from: http://its.syr.edu/web/ [Accessed 23rd March 2007].

- Taylor, M.J. and England, D. (2006) Internet Marketing: Web Site Navigational Design Issues. *Marketing Intelligence & Planning*, 24(1), p.77-85. Available from: http://www.emeraldinsight.com/Insight/ViewContentServlet?Filename=Published/Em eraldFullTextArticle/Articles/0200240106.html [Accessed 20th March 2007].

- Tiago, Maria *et al.* (2007) International Reality of Internet Use as Marketing Tool. *Journal of American Academy of Business*, 11(1), p.138-144. Available from: http://proquest.umi.com/pqdweb?index=0&did=1186428261&SrchMode=1&sid=1&F mt=4&VInst=PROD&VType=PQD&RQT=309&VName=PQD&TS=1175191275&cl ientId=57096 [Accessed 20th March 2007].

Lightning Source UK Ltd.
Milton Keynes UK
UKOW041816191012

200882UK00001B/128/P